GET WELL
WISHES

Also by June Cotner

Amazing Graces
Animal Blessings
Back to Joy
Baby Blessings
Bedside Prayers
Bless the Beasts
Bless the Day
Christmas Blessings
Comfort Prayers
Dog Blessings
Family Celebrations
Forever in Love
Garden Blessings
Graces
Gratitude Prayers
Heal Your Soul, Heal the World
The Home Design Handbook
House Blessings
Looking for God in All the Right Places
Miracles of Motherhood
Mothers and Daughters
Pocket Prayers
Say a Little Prayer: A Journal
Serenity Prayers
SOAR! Follow Your Dreams
Teen Sunshine Reflections
To Have and To Hold
Toasts
Wedding Blessings

GET WELL WISHES

PRAYERS AND POEMS FOR COMFORT AND HEALING

BY JUNE COTNER
FOREWORD BY ALLEN KLEIN

Published in the United States by Viva Editions, an imprint of Start Midnight, LLC, 375 Hudson Street, Twelfth Floor, New York, New York 10014.

Printed in the United States.
Cover design: Scott Idleman/Blink
Cover photograph: Lyn Randle/Getty Images
Text design: Frank Wiedemann

First Edition.
10 9 8 7 6 5 4 3 2 1

Trade paper ISBN: 978-1-63228-006-0
E-book ISBN: 978-1-63228-012-1

Library of Congress Cataloging-in-Publication Data is available.

DEDICATION

Get Well Wishes
is dedicated in memoriam to my dear friend
who inspired all who knew him:
Brian Cox
(1950-1999)

This book is also dedicated to my friends
who have fought or still fight the daily battles that illness entails:

Janine Canan,
Joanie Guggenmos,
and
Virginia Lynn Eathorne

I have great respect and admiration for your grit,
determination, and courage.
Thanks for helping me see that every day is truly a gift.
This book's for you...and please, be well.

Contents

eight | **INSPIRATION** 121

Foreword

Words are powerful. They can lift us up or bring us down.

If you doubt that, think of a time when somebody complimented you and told you how great you looked, or what a wonderful smile you had, or admired something you were wearing that day. How did that make you feel?

Think also about a time when you were ill, or perhaps in the hospital, and someone sent you a get-well card, emailed you some encouraging thoughts, or brought you some beautiful flowers. As ill as you might have been, probably those things lifted you up, even if just momentarily.

Get Well Wishes is like those encouraging words or the bouquet of flowers. It is a book of hope, healing, and heart. It is not only filled with prayers, poems, and prose but, more importantly, with love. It is the perfect gift to give to anyone who needs a little lift and lots of well wishes.

What is most impressive to me about this book is that it comes out of the author's own trials and tribulations—she had a serious car accident—and how powerful prayers, poems, and prose, like those in the book, helped her mend, get well, and get on with her life.

I, too, had a healing experience with some of the words printed within these covers. Last year I was in Israel to attend a wedding. It was a joyous occasion, but also a scary one. The ongoing conflict between Israel and the Palestinians flared up. Rockets were fired almost daily toward the town in which we were staying. What kept me feeling safe during that entire time was the "Prayer for Protection" that is in this book on page 14 and which I kept repeating every time I heard a missile approaching.

I like the selections the author has chosen as well as the varied categories she uses to contain those comforting words. The groupings include such things as courage, faith, and patience, among many others.

I also realized, while reading this book, that it is not only about get-well wishes for others but, in addition, it can be a powerful gift to give to yourself when you need some encouragement to rise above a situation, or when you are feeling down.

Even more than that, this inspiring book can be used in a totally different way than perhaps the author intended. It is not just a collection of get-well wishes but also a compendium of stay-well reminders illustrating that we have the power to create our own reality. One example is in the following writing, titled "What Really Counts" by Minister Joseph Fort Newton:

We cannot tell what may happen
to us in the strange medley of life.
But we can decide what happens in us,
how we take it, what we do with it—
and that is what really counts in the end.

Allen Klein
San Francisco
Author of *You Can't Ruin My Day* and *Change Your Life!*

Letter to Readers

Twenty years ago I started a collection of poems and prayers (some of which are included in this book) that helped me cope with a difficult journey that began with a car accident that changed my life. In one moment, my athletic lifestyle was transformed into a sedentary one. A neck injury changed me into a fragile, disabled woman. Just opening a window caused tremendous pain.

My medication made me lethargic and severely impacted my thinking process and memory—and there were many other unpleasant side effects to cope with. One of the prescriptions that was supposed to "help my nerve endings heal" was actually an antidepressant. When I quit using it cold turkey (not knowing it was an antidepressant), I sank into a depression, the state of a "lightless prison," which is so eloquently expressed by Arlene Gay Levine on page 74.

Three years later, I still couldn't ride my bicycle because the weight of a bicycle helmet was overwhelming. Sometimes the road to wellness can be a long one—one that requires more than physical stamina to complete the journey.

I have arranged the chapters in *Get Well Wishes* in an order that has personal significance for me. I found that when an accident or illness strikes, we first need comfort—from whatever source, hopefully from relatives and friends. But, in those "3 AM" moments (see page 22), when we feel most alone, often it is faith that helps pull us through our despair. Once we are strengthened by faith, we are fortified to move on toward rebuilding our lives.

But, oh, those initial steps are so difficult—when giving up seems to be the easier path. May the selections in "Courage" offer a stepping stone to start you on your road to discovering hope. For hope buoys our spirits, brings us optimism, and encourages us to go on so that the process of healing can begin.

As we improve, it's natural to reflect on the impact of the accident or illness on our lives. It's a time of great contemplation. Shortly after my accident, it seemed that all I could do was bemoan all I had lost. The words in my own prayer on page 134 gradually found their way into my soul—and as odd as it may seem, I began to experience glimmers of gratitude.

Gratitude sets the stage for inspiration. For me, I found that my period of great physical inactivity led to a surprising burst of mental activity that eventually resulted in my writing career. I seriously doubt that the "pre-accident June" would have slowed down enough to take on the writing projects I enjoy today.

We never know what curves life will throw at us. I hope the prayers, poems, and blessings in this book will bring you comfort, faith, courage, hope, healing, reflection, gratitude, and inspiration on your personal journey of recovery. Many have made the journey before you, but no one has experienced exactly what you are experiencing right now. May God's grace be with you. And may you be well.

June Cotner
P.O. Box 2765
Poulsbo, WA 98370
www.junecotner.com

Key for Bible translations used in *Get Well Wishes:*

GNT: Good News Translation
KJV: King James Version
NAB: New American Bible
NEV: New European Version
NIV: New International Version
TEV: Today's English Version

Thanks

I'm enormously grateful to Brenda Knight, publisher at Viva Editions for realizing the true potential of this book. I also appreciate the terrific support and help I have received from the staff at Viva: Kara Wuest, managing editor; Cat Snell, publishing associate; and Samantha Kornblum, marketing and editorial associate.

I so appreciate the guidance, enthusiasm, and creativity of my two agents, Denise Marcil and Anne Marie O'Farrell, at Marcil-O'Farrell Literary.

My husband Jim, my children Kyle and Kirsten, my sister Sue, and my closest friends continue to be a constant source of strength and support. You each enrich my life in so many ways and I can't thank you enough.

None of my books would be possible without the poets and writers who contribute their eloquent, insightful words to my collections. In addition to receiving several thousand submissions for each book, over nine-hundred poets and writers contribute to my books on a regular basis. I always know that when I sit down to read your submissions I will be deeply moved and inspired. Your words truly help me to be a better person!

Beginning with my first anthology, *Graces*, I used a "test market" group to help ensure that the selections were accessible to the general reader, inclusive enough to meet the satisfaction of three major religious beliefs, and poetic enough to please poets. To that end, I wish to thank the following individuals for participating in this process: Denise Marcil, my agent; Patrick Tracy, MD; Janine Canan, MD (also one of my longtime contributing poets); and Ann Cotner, RN.

Representing three major religions, I also wish to thank Father Paul Keenan, Rabbi Rami M. Shapiro, and Reverend Gary W. Huffman.

Deepest gratitude is owed to the following poets who lent their poetic talent to this project and gave me a careful critique: Barbara Crooker, Lori Eberhardy, Margaret Anne Huffman, Arlene Gay Levine, and Paula Timpson.

The highest recognition is owed to the poets whose work appears in *Get Well Wishes*. Your selections were chosen from thousands, and then had to meet the additional approval of my thirty-person "test market" group. I'd also like to pay respect to the thousands of poets who submit for my projects, but whose work wasn't included—often due to page number restrictions. Your poems help enrich my life every day; I wish I could publish all of you! Please know that your words have sparked a reverberation in the universe. As poetry anthologist Kate Farrell states: "What poets and artists do lives after them and adds something to the world, becoming a sort of man-made natural resource, a permanent public repository of private visions of the many different ways human life has been and is and might be."

I am enormously grateful for the following friends, relatives, and colleagues who participated in my "test market" process: Virginia Lynn Eathorne, Brian Cox, Marjorie Retzloff, Cheryl Edmonson, Sue Gitch, Jim Graves, Joanie Guggenmos, Patricia Huckell, Charlotte Carter Izett, Irma Kalman, Barb Krell, Lacey Menne, Kirsten Casey, Sue Peterson, and John Standish. Your feedback was so helpful to me!

I wouldn't have the opportunity to continue to do this work I love without the readers who purchase my books. Thank you for your support that now has extended over two decades!

And above all, I'm grateful to God for work that brings continual joy to my life, and for helping me see that each day is a blessing.

one
COMFORT

I will turn their mourning into gladness;
I will give them comfort and joy instead of sorrow.

—JEREMIAH 31:13 (NIV)

DO NOT BE AFRAID

Do not be afraid—I will save you.

I have called you by name—you are mine.

When you pass through deep waters,

I will be with you; your troubles will not overwhelm you.

—ISAIAH 43: 1–2 (TEV)

STILL WATERS

May still waters surround you
in a harbor of peace.
Think dragonflies on summer afternoons,
cow and calf in farmer's field;
think summer sunsets,
autumn moons,
fog mist on morning ponds.
Think still waters
and find quiet rest
among the thoughts
of family and friends
who wish for you—
gentle love—
always.

—PATRICIA M. POLAND

ANGEL PROMISE

Wherever you are
I will be there,
Whatever might help
I can bring.
Dark hours alone
need not frighten,
Whatever will soothe
I shall sing.

—SARA SANDERSON (1938–2014)

FROM YOUR FRIEND

For you I will pray—
every morning,
every morning and day,
every morning, day and night;
and every time God
brings you to mind,
and every time in between that.
Just know, I will be praying—
without ceasing...

—JILL NOBLIT MACGREGOR

UNENDING LOVE

We are loved
by an unending love.
We are embraced
by arms that find us
even when
we are hidden from ourselves.
We are touched
by fingers that soothe us
even when
we are too proud for soothing.
We are counseled
by voices that guide us
even when
we are too embittered to hear.
We are loved
by an unending love.
We are supported
by hands that uplift us
even in
the midst of a fall.
We are urged on
by eyes that meet us
even when

we are too weak for meeting.
We are loved
by an unending love.

—RABBI RAMI M. SHAPIRO

TO A DEAR FRIEND

Take my hand—it will not weaken me
Feel my warmth—it will not lessen
Touch my soul—it is there to be reached
Drink from my cup—there is always more
Absorb my caring—I feel part of your loss
Be strong in my strength—there's more than enough

—GWEN TREMAIN RUNYARD (1922–2013)

BREATHE DEEPLY

Breathe deeply—
know that I am here.

—NANCY TUPPER LING

ANGEL EMBRACE

There are angels who sit quietly
and whisper when we need comfort.
There are those who breathe life into us
when we are breathless.

There are angels who fill us with gracious support
when our souls become fragile,
and those who kiss us goodnight for a peaceful slumber.

There are angels that touch us with sacred laughter
when tears become a burden.
There are those who wrap their wings around us
and rock us until the ache in our heart disappears.

There are angels that can send us flying with wonder
when our hope begins to fade,
and those who devote everything to give us
everlasting peace in heaven.

—LORI EBERHARDY

EACH DAY YOU CALL MY HEART, O GOD

Each day You call my heart, O God.
I hear You in the silver
afternoons of winter,
the winds that play like harps
in leafless trees. I hear You
in the snow that walks
like shoes of pearl in darkness
and in light. You keep me
company in every kind of loneliness.
In sickness
and in health You walk with me.
I hold Your stars inside my soul.
Each day You call my heart, O God,
For You are always near.

—MARION SCHOEBERLEIN

A QUIET COMFORT

I look up to the sky and I see
one star shining brightly.
I know it is you.

The breeze whispers in my ear,
"You are not alone. I am here with you."

I find comfort as your light shines on me
and covers me with a warm embrace.
As the rhythm of life eases my burdens,
I feel completely held by your grace.

—LORI EBERHARDY

TESTING, TESTING...

Such a simple phrase, "Let's run a few tests," and here I am, O God, shivering, flimsy-gowned and alone, as scared of the tests as of their findings.

While I wait, cradle me as the wailing, lost child I've become. Closing my eyes and breathing deeply, I feel Your warming presence as a blanket tossed around my shoulders and know that no matter the bottom line being tallied up behind lead screens and computer consoles, You hold the most important truth, whispering it now, "You are my beloved child...I am with you."

—MARGARET ANNE HUFFMAN (1941–2000)

THE LORD IS MY SHEPHERD

The Lord is my shepherd; I shall not want. He maketh me to lie down in green pastures: he leadeth me beside the still waters. He restoreth my soul: he leadeth me in the paths of righteousness for his name's sake. Yea, though I walk through the valley of the shadow of death, I will fear no evil: for thou art with me; thy rod and thy staff they comfort me. Thou preparest a table before me in the presence of mine enemies: thou anointest my head with oil; my cup runneth over. Surely goodness and mercy shall follow me all the days of my life: and I will dwell in the house of the Lord for ever.

—PSALMS 23:1-6 (KJV)

PRAYER FOR PROTECTION

The light of God surrounds us;
The love of God enfolds us;
The power of God protects us;
The presence of God watches over us.
Wherever I am, God is!

—JAMES DILLET FREEMAN (1912–2003)

IF

If we could only surrender
Our earthbound idea of things,
We would discover
That our wings
Have always been there.

—CORRINE DE WINTER

LET NOTHING DISTURB YOU

Let nothing disturb you;
Let nothing dismay you.
All things pass;
God never changes.
Patience attains
All it strives for.
The one who has God
Finds that nothing is lacking.
God alone suffices.

—TERESA OF AVILA (1515–1582)

PEACE I GIVE UNTO YOU

Peace I leave with you,
my peace I give unto you:
not as the world giveth,
give I unto you.
Let not your heart be troubled,
neither let it be afraid.

—JOHN 14:27 (KJV)

IF I COULD

I would pour light into a spoon,
Roll words of beauty into sweets,
Fill the world with singing birds,
Cartwheel through the heavens,
Or somersault up the stairs.
I would do anything, if I could,
For you to feel better again.

—INGRID GOFF-MAIDOFF

two

FAITH

Faith is taking the first step
even when you don't see
the whole staircase.

—DR. MARTIN LUTHER KING, JR. (1929–1968)

A LIFE JACKET

Life has a way of surprising us.
It does not behave the way we
planned or anticipated.
That is when we grab on to faith
and hang on to it
like a life jacket
until better days.

—PHYLLIS JOY DAVISON

TAKE MY HAND

Hand in hand, dear God, we will make it through this lonely valley of illness, for I will not be alone. I will feel You in the hands of those who hold mine, who rub my back, wipe my feverish face, count out pills and potions to ease and heal; in the deft touch of those who bind up and patch my ailing body; in the consoling, uplifting, encircling hugs and embrace of family and friends.

Already I feel You near and am assured that wherever I am on this path of illness, Your strong hand is there to guide and to hold.

—MARGARET ANNE HUFFMAN (1941–2000)

3 AM

There is a place where we are alone.

It's called 3 AM.

3 AM is when the pain meds wear off.

3 AM is when sleep deserts you.

3 AM is when the silent movie of your life begins to roll in front of your staring eyes.

3 AM is when the deep, bone deep, gut deep, heart-wrenching grief of the things you haven't yet done explodes like a grenade. The foolishnesses you've committed. The words you can't take back. The things you didn't do because of fear. Hah! What was that fear compared to dying?

But I'll tell you a mystery.

Right there. Right then. Right in the middle of 3 AM.

Beside all the pain, physical and emotional.

Next to the dread

In the midst of deep wrenching grief:

God was with me.

Right there. Right beside me.

A presence.

Always.

Lo, God is with me.
And, I am not alone.

—SYLVIA MASI

STEPS

As disappointments slowly,
quietly stack like fallen leaves,
as sorrow finds you
cold and still like ice groaning
on the surface of the frozen lake,
listen for that voice
that has no sound, beloved.
After the wind calls your name
it will whisper in still moments
the words you long for.
The answer, the direction
the steps that lead you home.

—JOAN SHROYER-KENO

GRACE

Grace
Slips in
Sunrise,
Lightness,
A cleansing wave
When I
Remember
I am
Held.

—INGRID GOFF-MAIDOFF

THE SKIES ARE FULL OF PROMISE

God of life, there are days when the burdens we carry chafe our
shoulders and wear us down; when the road seems dreary and endless,
the skies gray and threatening; when our lives have no music in them
and our hearts are lonely, and our souls have lost their courage. Flood
the path with light, we beseech you; turn our eyes to where the skies
are full of promise.

—ST. AUGUSTINE (354–430)

CHIPPEWA SONG

Sometimes I go about pitying myself,
and all the time
I am being carried on great winds across the sky.

—AUTHOR UNKNOWN

GREAT EXPECTATIONS

At times it is hard to see the light
through these shadows of doubt,
but there is hope in my soul.

With great expectations I reach past
the shadows that surround me.
I transcend the darkness and my spirit
becomes woven in the sunlight.

With tenderness I listen to the sweet
sounds of amazing grace,
and with the vision of a child,
I remind myself that
this is the day, the hour, the moment
to keep the faith.

—LORI EBERHARDY

BELIEVE

When you come to the edge
Of all the light you know,

And are about to step off
Into the darkness of the unknown,

Faith is knowing
One of two things will happen:

There will be something solid to stand on,
Or you will be taught how to fly.

—AUTHOR UNKNOWN

SAFE PASSAGE

The touch of your hand comforts me.
The sound of your voice calms me.
My spirit is eager to fly free.
To break away from this fear that has become
a burden to me.
At times I feel like a prisoner and this
fear is painted thick on the walls that surround me
So I find an open door and
on the other side is you.
I'm not surprised.
It's always you.
You tell me to take your hand.
You rescue me.

—LORI EBERHARDY

PRAYER IN TIME OF TROUBLE

God of Peace,
God of All Tranquility,

Be for us Light
in all our darknesses.

Be for us Calm
in every storm.

Be for us Stillness
in our turmoil.

Let us rest in You,
as a child in
a mother's arms;
a nested bird.

And let Your Grace
now rest upon us,
as moonlight rests
upon the water;
as soft rain
falls to rest
on thirsty ground.

Let Your Grace
now rest
like gentle rain
upon us.

—DEBORAH GORDON COOPER

I WILL NOT BE OVERCOME

I know that at times I will be troubled,
I know that at times I will be belabored,
I know that at times I will be disquieted,
but I believe that I will not be overcome. Amen.

—JULIAN OF NORWICH (1342–1419)

LIKE JACOB IN THE MORNING

Sometimes it's hard to see;
hard to hear; hard to be.
Little comfort in wondering if we
have brought it on ourselves.
Out there at such a distance,
made up of your own resistance,
even there it's love's existence
that the story tells.

So I will pray for you that with
all the things you're going through,
you may be found anew like
Jacob in the morning.
And may the angels, angels
carry you.

—JIM CROEGAERT

PSALM

"Let the morning bring me word of your unfailing love,
for I have put my trust in you.
Show me the way I should go,
for to you I entrust my life."
—Psalm 143:8 (NIV)

Let the morning sunlight
slanting through the blinds,
this wide white dawn, *bring me word*

of your unfailing love—a note
tucked under my coffee mug
or taped to the bathroom mirror
or slid beneath the wipers on my car—

for I have put my trust
in you, the two of us walking
shoulder to shoulder. *Show me*

the way I should go, your broad hand
resting lightly on the small of my back,
guiding me through
the doorway of another day.

—EMILY RUTH HAZEL

DO NOT LOSE HEART

Therefore we do not lose heart.
Though outwardly we are wasting away,
yet inwardly we are being renewed day by day.
For our light and momentary troubles
are achieving for us an eternal glory
that far outweighs them all.
So we fix our eyes not on what is seen,
but on what is unseen.
For what is seen is temporary,
but what is unseen is eternal.

—2 CORINTHIANS 4:16–18 (NEV)

REFLECTIONS ON FAITH

Ask, and you will receive; seek, and you will find; knock, and the door will be opened to you.

—MATTHEW 7:7 (GNT)

Only through *surrender*
do we fully embrace *faith*.

—CORRINE DE WINTER

It is in the darkness when I feel your presence;
it is in the silence when I hear you call my name.

—NANCY TUPPER LING

Contrary to what many believe,
doubt is not the opposite of faith,
it is an element of faith.

—REVEREND DALE E. TURNER (1917–2006)

Faith is the certainty that
from the thorns of the rosebush
will one day emerge
the most fragrant of blossoms.

—BARB MAYER

They are your protection
When life seems too hard to bear.
And though you feel alone at times,
The angels…they are there.

—LEIGH ENGEL

Listen for your angel's voice in music, in kind words,
and in loving thoughts.

—SUZANNE SIEGAL ZENKEL

three
COURAGE

You must find the place inside yourself
where nothing is impossible.

—DEEPAK CHOPRA

THIS DAY

I ask for courage
to greet the dawn.
I ask for friends
to surround me
when I feel alone.
I ask for a song
to fill the darkness,
and for a peace
that pacifies my soul.
And when I am fully spent,
I ask for grace to comfort another.

—NANCY TUPPER LING

GRACE

Grant me that
graceful moment
in which pain
becomes learning
and tragedy, survivorship.

Let my tears
be as a river
or a mighty sea
floating my soul
beyond this rocky shore.

—KATE ROBINSON

SO YOU MUSTN'T BE FRIGHTENED

So you mustn't be frightened…if a sadness rises in front of you, larger than any you have ever seen; if an anxiety, like light and cloud-shadows, moves over your hands and over everything you do. You must realize that something is happening to you, that life has not forgotten you, that it holds you in its hand and will not let you fall. Why do you want to shut out of your life any uneasiness, any misery, any depression, since after all you don't know what work these conditions are doing inside you? Why do you want to persecute yourself with the question of where all this is coming from and where it is going? Since you know, after all, that you are in the midst of transitions and you wished for nothing so much as to change. If there is anything unhealthy in your reactions, just bear in mind that sickness is the means by which an organism frees itself from what is alien; so one must simply help it to be sick, to have its whole sickness and to break out with it, since that is the way it gets better. In you…so much is happening now; you must be patient like someone who is sick, and confident like someone who is recovering; for perhaps you are both. And more: you are also the doctor, who has to watch over himself. But in every sickness there are many days when the doctor can do nothing but wait. And that is what you, insofar as you are your own doctor, must now do, more than anything else.

—RAINER MARIA RILKE (1875–1926)

TRANSLATED BY STEPHEN MITCHELL

FACING THE FACTS

We are pulled, Gentle One, like a turkey wishbone in this balancing act of illness. We ping-pong between accepting and denying, giving up and fighting. Give us strength to find and face facts, for there is freedom and power in knowledge. Help us understand that *accepting* is not throwing in the towel; rather, through grace, *accepting* is like going to the bank to withdraw our savings...our spiritual, mental, and physical resources. As we make the transaction, we know You are our endless, bottomless, forever source.

—MARGARET ANNE HUFFMAN (1941–2000)

A NEW SONG

I will sing a new song in the darkness.

—NANCY TUPPER LING

LETTING GO

Let go of the place that holds,
Let go of the place that flinches,
Let go of the place that controls,
Let go of the place that fears.
Just let the ground support me.
Listen, the wind is breathing in the trees.
Sensing the edge of soft and hard,
I follow the unseen path.
Walking in the dark night,
I practice faith,
building confidence in the unknown.
I practice courage,
accepting the vastness
of what I cannot see.

—STEPHANIE KAZA

AT PEACE

Be tough in the way a blade of grass is:
rooted, willing to lean,
and at peace with what is around it.

—NATALIE GOLDBERG

DO THE BEST

When we do the best we can,
we never know what miracles await.

—HELEN KELLER (1880–1968)

THE BEGINNING

There will come a time when
you believe everything is finished.
That will be the beginning.

—LOUIS L'AMOUR (1908–1988)

REFLECTIONS ON COURAGE

I do not want [my children] to think, as I once did,
that courage is the absence of fear.
Courage is the strength to act wisely
when we are most afraid...

—MARY FISHER

Courage is fear that has said its prayers.

—KARL BARTH

You gain strength, courage, and confidence by every experience in
which you really stop to look fear in the face. You are able to say to
yourself, "I lived through this horror. I can take the next thing that
comes along." You must do the thing you think you cannot do.

—ELEANOR ROOSEVELT (1884–1962)

From moment to moment one can bear much.

—TERESA OF AVILA (1515–1582)

GRIEF

When grief pours salt
into the wounds of life,
we must not hide from it.
We have to face its fury
head on, wrestle with its
clawing anguish,
back and forth,
between depression
and desolation,
so that the pain doesn't
metastasize into anger,
overflowing our eyes,
flooding our hearts.
Experience and express
the sorrow.
Choose to accept its sting,
knowing that time
will anesthetize, scar tissue
form over incisions,
not as pliable, perhaps,
but just as strong as before.

—SUSAN ROGERS NORTON

WHERE THERE IS...

Where there is courage—fear fades

Where there is trust—peace reigns

Where there is grace—forgiveness heals

Where there is love—mercy abounds

Where there is faith—endurance is possible

Where there is hope—the future beckons

—GWYNETH M. BLEDSOE

STUBBORN FAITH

There is every reason to give up and give in,
for this illness is rough.
When I falter, remind me that with You,
I am as resilient as violets
pushing up through pavement cracks.

—MARGARET ANNE HUFFMAN (1941–2000)

DO WHAT YOU CAN

Do what you can,
with what you've got,
where you are.

—THEODORE ROOSEVELT (1858–1919)

SOMEHOW

Life's struggle
can be puzzling now & then.

Somehow
at the most difficult times
we find wings to fly.

—CORRINE DE WINTER

four

HOPE

We must accept finite disappointment,
but never lose infinite hope.

—DR. MARTIN LUTHER KING, JR. (1920–1968)

HOPE WILL COME AGAIN

Soft, like an April breeze,
hope will come to you
again. She will fill your
night with her autumn
moon; her soft, clear light
will bathe your sky
of all anxiety. Now she
lies beneath your
thoughts so near, yet so
far; but she will
come to you again! She will
fill your darkened
cloud with her crimson ray.
She will climb your
inner sky on silver wing:
and high above,
beyond all thoughts or dreams,
she will lift her
weary head and sing in ecstasy!

—THOMAS L. REID

HANGING BY A THREAD

Recovery is slow, Gentle Healer, and we're discouraged, hopeless.
Raise our eyes to spiderwebs spun in a corner and remind us that no
hope is too small. It is of *kiven*, Hebrew for "hope: to twist or twine
like a spiderweb." This is the quality of hope—amazing strength that
looks at first like a fragile, insignificant strand. Yet think what it does
for the spider. Help us twist our tiny-strand hope into sturdy ropes of
commitment to taking the next, and the next step toward health.

—MARGARET ANNE HUFFMAN (1941–2000)

DON'T GIVE UP

Hope is what will get you through this—
the hope that you can beat it.
If you lose your hope, the illness has won.
Don't give up without a fight.

—KIRSTEN CASEY

PRAYER FROM A HOSPITAL BED

My God,
I am in this place not because I choose to be
but because I need to be.
My body is not working as it should.
Heal me, Lord.
I am weary of tests, of being poked and prodded.
Give me patience, Lord.
This can be a lonely place;
Be present with me, Lord.
Help me to remember your nearness,
to draw strength from your love
and hope from your promises.
Amen.

—JIM CROEGAERT

HOPE

Bring me hope
in bright brass urns
of monsoon rain,
between the claps of thunder
under thoughts that fill the ponds
and swell the river
Bring me hope
and I will bloom
like a lotus in sun.

—LALITA NORONHA

SOWING, REAPING

We *must* believe small healing steps matter, Great Encourager, for You say mountains can be budged with faith as small as mustard seeds. Ah, though, there's nothing small about a Scottish hillside blanketed with yellow mustard flowers. They are tiny *and* mighty—a package deal with You at our elbow. Forgive us when we don't recognize mustard-seed power in the small accomplishments we are making as we move from illness through recovery to restored health.

Too often, we confess, we wait for overnight drama and overlook tiny flickers of change. They're begging to be noticed and gathered into a radiant harvest of hope.

—MARGARET ANNE HUFFMAN (1941–2000)

SPRING IS MY FAITH

I ask in my fear
why this happened to me.
Yet I can't hold back
the praise that wells up inside.

I ask in my pain
why I must suffer.
Yet gratitude is the constant
motion within, and I know
the deep nourishment of spirit.

The cancer cells multiply
like flakes of snow.
My body is a waste of white.
Yet spring is my faith.
In the bright morning sun
the overnight snow glitters
and is gone.
The forsythia remains.

—IDA FASEL (1909–2012)

THE ESSENCE OF TOUCH

It's about the Spirit.
Where it goes.
Who it touches.
It holds us close and it sets us free.
We can choose to sit and wait
or we can stand and trust
that it will mend our broken wings and
welcome our lost souls.
This invisible force gives us hope,
offers us comfort, whispers our salvation.
It invites us among the angels and gives us
the confidence to fly.

—LORI EBERHARDY

PRAY

Rejoice in hope,
endure in affliction,
persevere in prayer.

—ROMANS 12:12 (NAB)

Prayer,
with a dose of hope,
is the strongest medicine.

—BARB MAYER

AN ASSIGNMENT

One of the most effective ways to neutralize medical pessimism is to find someone who had the same problem you do and is now healed.

—ANDREW WEIL

PATIENCE

Help me look beyond the fence
caging my uneasy heart.

Help me listen for the gentle spirit
approaching softly.

Help me open the heavy gate
to allow its entry.

Help me welcome patience and
quiet my fears.

—SUSAN KOEFOD

THE TIDE WILL TURN

When you get into a tight place
and everything goes against you
'til it seems as though
you could not hang on a minute longer,
never give up then,
for that is just the place and time
that the tide will turn.

—HARRIET BEECHER STOWE (1811–1896)

The lowest ebb is the turn of the tide.

—HENRY WADSWORTH LONGFELLOW (1807–1882)

If you do not hope, you will not find what is beyond your hopes.

—ST. CLEMENT OF ALEXANDRIA (150–211)

FOR WE ARE HERE,

not merely
to bloom in the light,
but rather, like trees,
to be weathered:
burned by heat, frozen by snow;
and though our hearts
have been broken,
still, we put out new leaves
in spring,
begin again.

—BARBARA CROOKER

REJOICE

And we rejoice in the hope of the glory of God.
Not only so, but we also rejoice in our sufferings,
because we know that suffering produces perseverance;
perseverance, character
and character, hope.

—ROMANS 5:2–4 (NIV)

HOPING

Hoping is knowing that there is love,
it is trust in tomorrow
it is falling asleep
and waking again
when the sun rises.
In the midst of a gale at sea,
it is to discover land.
In the eyes of another
it is to see that he understands you...
As long as there still is hope
There will also be prayer...
And God will be holding you
in his hands.

—AUTHOR UNKNOWN

five

HEALING

Never underestimate
the healing effects of beauty.

—FLORENCE NIGHTINGALE (1820–1910)

RX

Right after the diagnosis, "You're sick," comes the blissful command, "Go to bed." No guilt. No argument. Just go to bed. Lie on white sheets. Sleep. Rouse and read a chapter of your book. Nap. Awaken to a cooler forehead and sip chamomile tea poured from the chubby brown pot. Doze. Say little. Listen to the rustle of your turning on the sheets, the rustle of pages as you read another chapter, the rustle of loved ones being quiet downstairs. The quiet is for you. Get well.

—MARTHA K. BAKER

TWILIGHT CURE

Hush, this is the soft hour
Let us settle down
Hush, this is the cadence of peace
Let us breathe deeply
Hush, this is the healing time
Let us go within
Hush, this is the prayer
Let us convalesce.

—ARLENE GAY LEVINE

IN THE HOUSE OF THE SUN

In the house of the sun there is
A yellow just for you; it shines
Even brighter when you are
Not looking or waiting.
In the house of the moon there is
A white just for you; it holds
Your worries, your fears, your wants;
It rocks them all to sleep.
In the house of your heart there are
So many colors we cannot count
Or name them; they swirl together
Endlessly healing, healing, healing.

—CASSIE PREMO STEELE

GET WELL

Get well as rivers running,
spirits dancing under blue, blue skies.
Listen to the rain.
Begin again.
Go to where rose blossoms
drift into your heart and
nights are no longer too long.
Believe you can dance
in the darkness—
nothing will overshadow
your life.
God is with you in every moment in time.
Celebrate seaside moments
of peace
love
and joy
that echo your name
and hold your hand
the same way God does.
Get well.

—PAULA TIMPSON

SANCTUARY

Close your eyes.
Grab hold of your imagination.
Tug on it 'til it cooperates, and
with its help, create a haven,
your own private sanctuary,
where you can escape to
for solace, courage
or strength of body and soul.

It could be a sheltered green garden,
a wooded glen or pebbled beach,
whatever scene nourishes you,
whatever sights and sounds calm you,
whatever regenerates you.

Know that in the blink of an eye,
the tick of a heart's clock,
you can go there.
Airline tickets aren't necessary.
Road maps can be stored away.
Advanced booking not required.
The only reservation you need make
is with yourself.

—SUSAN ROGERS NORTON

FOR HEALING

May we discover through pain and torment, the strength to live with
   grace and humor.
May we discover through doubt and anguish, the strength to live
   with dignity and holiness.
May we discover through suffering and fear, the strength to move
   toward healing.

May it come to pass that we be restored to health and to vigor.
May Life grant us wellness of body, spirit, and mind.
And if this cannot be so, may we find in this transformation and
   passage
moments of meaning, opportunities for love
and the deep and gracious calm that comes when we allow ourselves
   to move on.

—RABBI RAMI M. SHAPIRO

THIS I KNOW

The wound: flesh or spirit deep
The choice: to quit or keep on
The way: accept and let go
The promise: to heal and grow

—ARLENE GAY LEVINE

WHY NOT?

In the face of fear
let me hope

In the face of doubt
let me know

In the grip of loneliness
let me reach out

In the grip of pain
let me breathe

In spite of grief
let me smile

In spite of anger
let me pray

—MARYANNE HANNAN

WOMAN TO WOMAN

I am no stranger.
I am a woman like you
mending after illness.
I would take the fear
palpable as a walnut
out of your body,
the fear that something
can erase our breath.
Somewhere inside
a wisdom larger than us
knows the course of our lives
and carries the weight
of our pain and fear,
and offers with tender hands
the faith and understanding
that leads to healing.

—MARIAN OLSON

FOR A DEAR ONE AT A DARK TIME

Your world seems empty now: a puzzle with pieces
you thought made you complete, now missing.
If I could make you listen, in your loneliest hour,
the doves continue to coo and soft breezes
still strum their spring song on budding branches.
If I could help you see, in your lightless prison,
the perfection of a powder-blue-sky day
has not gone away and the courageous yellow face
of a solitary dandelion defies the gardener's rake.

If I could urge you to inhale, despite your clenched chest,
you'd be healed by the green tonic of mown grass
or even the humble aroma of a potato
baking in the oven just for you.
If I could I would teach you to taste the salt of your tears
and explore their source, to feel the jagged edges
of your newly broken heart, and with those same hands,
use the thread of your pain to sew a stronger version
whole again.

—ARLENE GAY LEVINE

REFLECTIONS ON HEALING

A merry heart doeth good
like a medicine.

—PROVERBS 17:22 (KJV)

Healing is not only a question of time;
it's a question of outlook.

—BARB MAYER

Healing does not mean going back to the way things were before,
but rather allowing what is now to move us closer to God.

—RAM DASS

Honor the healing power of nature.

—HIPPOCRATES (CA. 460–377 B.C.E.)

NOW

Now is not the time
to look for blame or reason.
It is not the time to tell yourself,
"I should have been, done, seen or known."
You have been working hard for so long,
and the body says, "now rest."
It is time for patience, self-love, cherishing,
gentleness and gathering in.
It is time to receive these gifts.
One day soon you will look back
with a deep and peaceful awareness:
The Infinite Goodness holds you,
even in anguish, fear and pain.
Yes: Love works in mysterious ways.

—INGRID GOFF-MAIDOFF

LIVE QUIETLY

God help us to live quietly
Amidst the clamor,
To find that slower pace
that gentler place
Where our hearts can listen,
Where we can listen to
Our hearts.
Amen.

—JIM CROEGAERT

TAKE TIME

Take time to relax,
take time to reflect,
take time to heal.

—BARB MAYER

BE PATIENT

Of course you are anxious to feel better, but don't be impatient. Healing takes time. Despite great advances in medicine, the biggest part of your recovery is attributable to the enormous healing power inside you. The body heals itself according to its own timetable—anxious thoughts never hasten recuperation.

—CRISWELL FREEMAN

THE BEST CURE

The best cure for the body
is to quiet the mind.

—NAPOLEON BONAPARTE (1769–1821)

RENAISSANCE

Coming back to life
like the earth in spring,
energy flows
in a gentle resurgence
throughout my being.

Coming back to life,
my long-smoldering soul
is all aflame, rekindled
by a tender touch
and time.

—ABIGAIL BRANDT

FOR A FRIEND LYING IN INTENSIVE CARE WAITING FOR HER WHITE BLOOD CELLS TO REJUVENATE AFTER A BONE-MARROW TRANSPLANT

The jonquils. They come back. They split the earth with
their green swords, bearing cups of light.
The forsythia comes back, spraying its thin whips with
blossom, one loud yellow shout.
The robins. They come back. They pull the sun on the
silver thread of their song.
The iris come back. They dance in the soft air in silken
gowns of midnight blue.
The lilacs come back. They trail their perfume like a scarf
of violet chiffon.
And the leaves come back, on every tree and bush, millions
and millions of small green hands applauding your return.

—BARBARA CROOKER

ANGEL WINGS

Wrap yourself in angel wings,
Settling deep within strength and solace.
Wrap yourself in angel wings,
Composed in a graceful tune to life.
Be comforted,
Be guarded,
Be well.

—ANNIE DOUGHERTY

A THOUSAND ANGELS

I send a thousand healing angels,
each one watching over you as gently
as the waves caress the shore,
each one whispering *I love you*
a hundred thousand times, and more.

As you go under, know that they are there,
guiding your surgeon's mind, her hands and heart;
and as you wake from the ether of your sleep,
listen for their song, accept their art:

They will be bending over you and singing, *heal, heal,*
their voices a choir of jubilant bells,
their wings a flutter of doves,
each note swelling with love.

—MICHAEL S. GLASER

SINK INTO STILLNESS

As you close your eyes,
sink into stillness.
Let these periods of rest and respite
reassure your mind
that all its frantic fantasies
were but the dreams
of fever that has passed away.
Let it be still
and thankfully accept its healing.
No more fearful dreams will come,
now that you rest in God.

—A COURSE IN MIRACLES

SURRENDER TO WONDER

In Wonder was I conceived
and in Wonder have I found my being.
Thus I call upon you, the Source of Wonder
to open my heart to healing.

In you I discover the mystery of Life
and the necessity of Death.
In you I see all things and their opposites
not as warring parties
but as partners in a dance
whose rhythm is none other
than the beating of my own soul.

Denial may come, but so too will acceptance.
Anger may come, but so too will calm.
I have bargained with my fears
and found them unwilling to compromise.
So now I turn to you,
to the Wonder that is my True Nature.

My tears will pass
and so will my laughter.
But I will not be silenced,

for I will sing praises of Wonder
through sickness and health;
knowing that in the end,
this too shall pass.

—RABBI RAMI M. SHAPIRO

six

REFLECTIONS

Small graces come to us in unexpected places.
Many great things are born from dark places.

—CORRINE DE WINTER

I LIVE IN WONDER

I live in wonder
of my own frailty and
the simple ways it teaches me
to be still.

I breathe the gentle whisper
of patience learned at rest
on the sea, becalmed.

Land and feet will meet again,
no hurry. I float in
the shimmering
stillness, marveling
at how fragile, and yet
how seaworthy,
I have become.

—PAMELA BURKE

IN THE MIDST OF GREATEST SORROW

It is a mark of faith, nobility and courage
to turn a minus into a plus and to discover positive
good in the midst of greatest sorrow.

—REVEREND DALE E. TURNER (1917–2006)

HOW TO ENDURE PAIN

Having four years ago gone through stage 3/4 cancer, my experience
has been that within pain, there is usually a nugget of an evolution of
a new consciousness. See whatever you're going through as something
that can be about your enlightenment as opposed to a pointless horror.

—EVE ENSLER

TOMORROW

It has often been said that in our lives
There are seasons for all things.
To laugh, to love, to share our joy
And the happiness life brings.

But there are times when darkness comes
And shadows the fragile heart.
We courageously fight and silently pray
For our healing time to start.

It is at these moments when our lives are filled
With pain or strife or sorrow
That God's gracious understanding is revealed
In a gift we call "tomorrow."

A new day brimming with possibilities
And hope sent from above,
Bestowed to help ease the cross we bear
With Heaven's unbending love.

—HEATHER BERRY

IN THE MIDST OF PAIN

My chemotherapy is at a difficult point.
I am tired of being tired and sick.
Since I have so little energy, I try to focus on small pleasures
so that I feel like I still have a life and the disease is not taking over.

When I don't accomplish as much as I want,
I find myself angry at life
and jealous of those who can do what I do not have the energy for,
trying hard not to let this hideous disease control me.
I fight melancholy on a daily basis.
It's a struggle to live on the bright side of life
when I don't have the energy to lift a dust rag.

The will to heal comes from within.
To question illness leads to confusion and despair.
To accept the gamble of life brings understanding
and appreciation of what it is to live.
I resent pity because so many suffer more than I do.

I have truly lived my life fully.
Most people live without disease and its consequences
but many of them don't live as full a life as those who are ill.
We, who struggle daily, appreciate all that we have.

—VIRGINIA LYNN EATHORNE

PAIN

When we must live with pain
that dark-robed visitor
becomes more bearable
as it grows more familiar.
We begin to sense how long
we must endure its presence,
we understand when to struggle
against its grim power
and when to submit.
Through pain we learn about
our bodies and our spirits.
Pain cleanses us, the edge
of its robe sweeping away
regret, confusion, and pettiness.
And when pain parts from us,
releasing us from its grip,
we are left empty, purified,
and grateful for small pleasures.

—SUZANNE C. COLE

THE BEST WE CAN DO

A rose bush wilting in July heat
does not blame the earth, lets its roots
search deep for the waters of life.
After its surge of golden glory
the bare oak does not accuse
the winter's frigid air, invites
the wind to sing hymns through
its naked boughs.

The best we can do is to allow,
learn to love the changing
landscape of our lives.
Episodes of dark and doubt
are unexpected guests, asking only
to be welcomed for a while,
these gods in disguise
who guide us home.

—ARLENE GAY LEVINE

PERMANENT GIFTS

Sometimes
the presence of God
sweeps through us
like a gust of autumn wind
stripping away
what we thought was essential.

The golden leaves of our lives
lie scattered at our feet
and we are left
looking at the bare trunk
of our existence.

In this stripping
we touch the core of who we are
and know we will survive the winter.

It is only through this loss
that we discover
what we can never lose.

—MOLLY SRODE

HOPE FROM A CANCER SURVIVOR

I gave up innocence
for all of this—
a life without guarantees,
but in exchange
I planted the seeds
of eternity,
in trust and belief,
in homage to grief,
in the endless renewability
of surrender.

—SUSAN MOON

LINES IN THE SAND

When the tide is high, the sand is submerged
The shells and seaweed wash back out to sea
Sandcastles slump into heaps and soon vanish
Our footprints, wiped out, leave no trace
The messages drawn with our fingers—gone

A new day dawns and the tide has now ebbed
Bright colored stones sparkle in sunlight
Sandpipers trip back and forth digging up treasures
We tread in soft sand, beyond reach of the ocean
And write a new message, one that will last

We have learned from yesterday's losses
To stand and withstand the high tides and low tides
The waves cannot touch the memories we cherish
Or erase the beauty of those who walked with us
Our message, the same—we loved and were loved

—GWYNETH M. BLEDSOE

A MEDITATION ON ACCEPTANCE

Whatever is in harmony with you, O Universe,
is in harmony with me.
Whatever comes in due season for you
is not too early or too late for me.
What your seasons bring is fruit for me,
for all things come from you and return to you.

—MARCUS AURELIUS (121 AD–180 AD)

MEDITATIONS, BOOK IV, 23

TRANSLATED BY MARYANNE HANNAN

WHAT REALLY COUNTS

We cannot tell what may happen
to us in the strange medley of life.
But we can decide what happens in us,
how we take it, what we do with it—
and that is what really counts in the end.

—JOSEPH FORT NEWTON (1876–1950)

THE FINAL SCORE

The final score is more than how
We won or lost with pride;
It's how we played the game of life
With laughter on our side.

—CHARLES GHIGNA

THE SOURCES OF HUMAN STRENGTH

Suffering and sorrow remain the supreme mystery of life. A great source of steadiness can be found in the knowledge that countless others have faced precisely the same problems without being utterly defeated in spirit. No wound of the body or soul is unique or entirely new, and others with similar scars have something to say to us. Among the sources of human strength is a resource unequaled—the friendship of any person who has preceded another through a similar valley who can quietly say, "I understand."

—REVEREND DALE E. TURNER (1917–2006)

IN SICKNESS

It is in sickness
(not in health)
that our true nature
shows its face,
shines a light
upon our shadowy
still-beating hearts.

You have risen
up out of darkness
to see this truth.
You are a brave dancer
moving your body
to the music
God continues to make.

—PETER MARKUS

SWEET CHILD,

I want to carry
all of this for you…
the needle pricks,
the trail of tubes,
the wakeful nights,
but you sit on your bed,
folding tiny red hearts
for your hospital friends,
and I know the wideness
of your heart is immeasurable.

—NANCY TUPPER LING

STEADFAST HOPE

Out of times
of tremendous trial
sprout seasons
of abundant
growth.

—JOAN MARIE ARBOGAST

DIFFICULTIES

Difficulties are God's errands and trainers, and only through them can
one come to the fullness of humanity.

—HENRY WARD BEECHER (1813–1887)

THE JOURNEY

Spring knows that Winter
is part of the journey.

—SALLY CLARK

THE WAY OF ALL FLESH

The beginning is new
Fresh with promise

The middle is ours
To wrest meaning from pain
Comfort from confusion

The end is forgiveness
In the end is Love

—MARYANNE HANNAN

OUR WAY

Our way is not soft grass,
it's a mountain path
with lots of rocks.
But it goes upwards,
forward, toward the sun.

—RUTH WESTHEIMER

REFLECTIONS

God spoke today in flowers,
And I, who was waiting on words,
Almost missed the conversation.

—INGRID GOFF-MAIDOFF

Listening to the birds can be a meditation
if you listen with awareness.

—OSHO

Some of life's deepest insights and larger truths are ushered into our
lives by pain and sorrow. Again and again, we come to see that great
lives sing most gloriously when assaulted by the winds of adversity.

—REVEREND DALE E. TURNER (1917–2006)

All suffering prepares the soul for vision.

—MARTIN BUBER (1878–1965)

The longer we dwell on our misfortunes, the greater is their power to harm us.

—VOLTAIRE (1694–1778)

The remedy against bad times
is to have patience with them.

—ARABIC PROVERB

Serenity comes not alone by removing the outward causes and occasions of fear, but by the discovery of inward reservoirs to draw upon.

—RUFUS M. JONES

Life cannot be choreographed,
but we can learn to improvise.

—EMILY RUTH HAZEL

ATTITUDE

The greatest discovery of my generation is that a human being can alter his life by altering the attitude of his mind.

—WILLIAM JAMES (1842–1910)

BE CURIOUS

rather than critical.
A hint of smile
opens the heart
better than a closed mind
which furrows the brow.

—JOYCE LOMBARD

REFLECT

Reflect on the dark
where fear is lost.

Reflect on the dark
where light begins.

Reflect on the dark
where gold is dancing.

—JANINE CANAN

seven

GRATITUDE

Gratitude makes sense of our past,
brings peace for today,
and creates a vision for tomorrow.

—MELODY BEATTIE

THE GUEST HOUSE

This being human is a guest house.
Every morning a new arrival.

A joy, a depression, a meanness,
some momentary awareness comes
as an unexpected visitor.

Welcome and entertain them all!
Even if they're a crowd of sorrows,
who violently sweep your house
empty of its furniture,
still, treat each guest honorably.
He may be clearing you out
for some new delight.

The dark thought, the shame, the malice,
meet them at the door laughing,
and invite them in.

Be grateful for whoever comes,
because each has been sent
as a guide from beyond.

—RUMI (1207–1273)

TRANSLATED BY COLEMAN BARKS

PEACE BEGINS WITHIN

Sometimes it's the little things that mean the most: the song of a bird, a warm breeze blowing through the trees, a friendly voice on the other end of a telephone, a note written by a friend to us when we need encouragement, the wag of a dog's tail as we come home from a hard day at work. These things are intangible—we cannot put a price tag on what they mean to us or how they help us to feel abiding peace even in the midst of turmoil. When I am tempted to lose control and get angry or bitter, I must remember the things which make me happy, and become peaceful within. No matter what the outward appearances, I can always return to these things, and feel the joy that comes from them.

Today I am thankful for the little things that bring peace from within.

—HEATHER PARKINS

TO THE GARDENER OF THE WORLD

Thank you for arousing in us
a hunger to live,
for bringing us to rest
in the shade of your Tree of Life,
for awakening in us
the light of your promise,
for breathing into our weary limbs
your spirit of refreshment and renewal.

—FATHER JOHN B. GIULIANI

UNKNOWN BLESSINGS

Give thanks
for unknown
blessings already
on their way.

—NATIVE AMERICAN SAYING

THE GIFTS OF ILLNESS

In illness I must slow down,
rest, treat myself with tenderness—
hard things to do sometimes
without the excuse, "I'm sick."
In illness I must rely on others;
exposing my vulnerability,
trusting others with my needs,
is good medicine for my soul.

Even in physical illness,
I can be spiritually healthy,
curious about the world,
and grateful for small gifts—
fresh crisp bed linens,
plump feather pillows
hand-squeezed orange juice,
chamomile tea and toast,
a book of prayers,
a call from a friend,
a rental movie I missed.

I didn't choose to be ill—but
I can choose to accept its gifts.

—SUZANNE C. COLE

A GOOD PROGNOSIS

It helps that I have a good prognosis; I focus on that and to listening to what I might learn from this experience. I am beginning to more fully appreciate each day as it unfolds, something that I have always strived for but could always be put off in the innocence of time stretched forever ahead of me. That innocence was shattered and I have to deal with that loss, but the gain from living more fully in the moment provides meaning. Thank you.

—SALLY ROSLOFF

SUFI SAYING

When the heart weeps for what it has lost,
The Spirit laughs for what it has found.

—AUTHOR UNKNOWN

RAINBOWS

A true sign of the miracles in God's world occurs when a rainbow appears, bright and shining, through the darkest of cloudy days. We have sought pots of gold at the end of them, and have watched them appear in waterfalls, crystals and other places. We never know when a rainbow will appear, and like the wonders of a rainbow full of its spectrum of color, we must remember that the one who made the rainbows beautiful also made us. We can be like a rainbow: full of color, shining through adversity.

Today I give thanks for the unique colors in my world, and give thanks that I am able to enjoy them.

—HEATHER PARKINS

SEE THE GOOD

Gratitude nourishes the heart as one chooses
to see the good in all things.

—REVEREND PHYLLIS ANN MIN

DIVINE GIFTS

Life is so generous a giver, but we, judging its gifts by their covering,
cast them away as ugly or heavy, or hard. Remove the covering,
and you will find beneath it a living splendor, woven of love,
by wisdom, with power.

Welcome it, grasp it, and you touch the angel's hand that brings it
    to you.
Everything we call a trial, a sorrow or a duty, believe me,
that angel's hand is there; the gift is there, and the wonder of an
    overshadowing presence. Our joys too: be not content with them
    as joys.
They too conceal diviner gifts.

—FRA GIOVANNI GIOCONDO (C. 1433–1515)

SO VERY BLESSED

Cancer is such a weird thing…
it has taught me each day is a gift
that cannot be taken for granted.
We feel so lucky, so fortunate, and so very blessed.
We live each day and love each moment.

—JOANIE GUGGENMOS

GRATITUDE

The feeling of gratitude puts life in perspective.
The expression of gratitude
allows us to share that perspective with others.

—BARB MAYER

FOR SUCH A TIME AS THIS

Blessed is she who,
In the midst of her own pain,
Reaches out to comfort others
With that comfort which she, herself, has received.

Blessed is she who shares in the cup of suffering,
Yet offers a taste of the bread of life
To those who will accept it.

Blessed is she who reaches out,
Across the waiting room,
To the bed on the other side of the curtain,
To share words of faith and visions of heaven.

Blessed is she who realizes that
Her circumstances may have been ordained
For such a time as this.

—SUSANNE WIGGINS BUNCH

BLESSED

Blessed be the doctor who listens to my fears.
Blessed be the nurse who wipes my brow.
Blessed be the aide who changes my sheets.
Blessed be the friend who colors my room with flowers.
Blessed are you, for you have met me where I am.

—NANCY TUPPER LING

DEAR FRIEND,

I will not ask what I can do for you today;
instead, I will sit by your side
and hold your hand.

—NANCY TUPPER LING

YOUR MONUMENTAL KINDNESS

I was wounded, and you took me into your heart.
I was lost, and you led me along.
I was broken, and you reached out a hand.

—SUSAN LANDON

EVERYONE IS BLESSED

When we give cheerfully
and accept gracefully,
everyone is blessed.

—MAYA ANGELOU (1928–2014)

eight

INSPIRATION

Learn from yesterday,
live for today,
hope for tomorrow.

—ALBERT EINSTEIN (1879–1955)

MAY YOU BE WELL

May the morning sun shine in your heart.
May the blue-white sky
be in
all your days.
May the moon and the stars
shine on all your nights.
Delight yourself.
God's gifts
are yours
every day.
May quiet smiles brighten you.
May you be well.

—PAULA TIMPSON

STAY WELL

Let your soul create
a sanctuary where
all dreams are possible
and life is grand as God's glory.
The beach stretches
before you.
You are strong as the sea's song.
Whitecaps travel and return.
May you never
feel alone or
lose sight of the
sacred seasons of your soul.
Stay well.

—PAULA TIMPSON

ONE YEAR TO LIVE

If I had but one year to live;
One year to help; one year to give;
One year to love; one year to bless;
One year of better things to stress;
One year to sing; one year to smile;
To brighten earth a little while;
I think that I would spend each day,
In just the very selfsame way
That I do now. For from afar
The call may come to cross the bar
At any time, and I must be
Prepared to meet eternity.
So if I have a year to live,
Or just a day in which to give
A pleasant smile, a helping hand,
A mind that tries to understand
A fellow-creature when in need,
'Tis one with me,—I take no heed;
But try to live each day He sends
To serve my gracious Master's ends.

—MARY DAVIS REED

BREAST CANCER BENEFIT

What matters is not the cancer.
Nor is it the bald head,
the misshapen blouse,
the scarred chest,
the ashen skin
that does not seem to fit
the sunken cheeks.

It is how these women laugh and nod
and agree about cancer
as if it is the daily news, a new joke,
an old truth;
how they tilt their head in a way
that says grace,
how they walk with an air that says
I am miraculous,
how their partners look as if
they might just be overcome with agony
and joy
if given just one more moment to watch
as these women bask in life.

—ROSIE MOLINARY

RESTING PLACE

Today is a resting place on my journey, Lord.
Today I'm relaxing my hold on worry,
loosening the ties that bind me to this illness
letting go of all my complaints and apprehension.
They can simmer on the back burner—provide tomorrow's stew.

Today I'm remembering
old friends—laughs and tears we shared;
old beaus—dancing in moonlight;
old days when my body and I had some wonderful times
enjoying sunshine, cool water, the treasures of the snow.

Hold my hand today, Lord, as I give thanks
for roses and babies and long swirly skirts;
for twinkling eyes and strong arms and soft voices—
for memories.

Hold my hand tomorrow, too, Lord.
Float me in the safe waters of Your love.

—JOAN EHEART CINELLI (1929–2015)

BEFORE IT IS TOO LATE

If you have a tender message,
Or a loving word to say,
Do not wait till you forget it,
But whisper it today;
The tender word unspoken,
The letter never sent,
The long-forgotten messages,
The wealth of love unspent—
For these some hearts are breaking,
For these some loved ones wait;
So show them that you care for them
Before it is too late.

—FRANK HERBERT SWEET

RESTORATION ZONE

In the aftermath of a major illness, it takes energy and courage to rebuild, Great Architect of our lives. How amazing that Your gift of courage translates *wishing* into *hoping*, the active word we need; it turns worry into energy and fear into determination.

Assure us that it's okay to be afraid, for fear is honest; so are anger, disappointment, grief. Help us recognize feelings as potential fuel that can be turned into reconstruction tools. Through Your grace, we've courageously faced *what is* and are now off to see *what can be*.

—MARGARET ANNE HUFFMAN (1941–2000)

WHAT CANCER CANNOT DO

Cancer is limited…

It cannot cripple love,
It cannot shatter hope,
It cannot erode faith,
It cannot destroy peace,
It cannot kill friendship,
It cannot suppress memories,
It cannot silence courage,
It cannot invade the soul,
It cannot steal eternal life,
It cannot conquer the spirit!

—AUTHOR UNKNOWN

REJOICE

This is the day which the Lord hath made;
we will rejoice and be glad in it.

—PSALMS 118:24 (KJV)

POSITIVE OUTLOOK

When we believe that the days ahead will be good days,
we move forward with confidence and hope,
and by such positive outlook,
we help to fulfill our expectations.

—REVEREND DALE E. TURNER (1917–2006)

TOMORROW IS NOT PROMISED

Tomorrow is not promised,
So I will live today
With faith, with joy, in peacefulness,
While death is held at bay.

I will not waste a moment of
Life's offerings and gifts;
These pieces of eternity
I'll use with care and thrift.

And yet I'll not be frugal with
The love that's mine to give,
But share with great abandon;
'Tis the only way *to live.*

—SUSANNE WIGGINS BUNCH

NO MATTER HOW LONG THE TRAIL

Dear Lord,
Make me brave
like the piñon pine
clinging to the crags,
and the Indian paintbrush
pushing through the rocks,
or the daisies
dancing near the trail.

Give me courage
like the penstemon
waving back the heat
and the claret cup
bursting forth
for just one day
or the cliff rose
challenging the buttes.

Let me be strong
in singular ways—
eager to press against stone,
unwavering in purpose
no matter the odds—

For every small splash of color
under the bleaching sky
brings hope to weary walkers,
lends lightness to faltering footsteps

Let me be bold
bright
blazing...
no matter how brief the day,
no matter how long the trail.

Amen

—TRISH KASPAR (1942–2013)

PERSPECTIVE

Rather than focusing
on what has been lost,
Dear God, help me to be grateful
for how much I still have.

—JUNE COTNER

A NEW DIMENSION

When we face a personal calamity and handle it well, we add a new dimension in our character. The pain and trouble we shrink from— and try to escape—when used wisely, often turns out to be the source of the best in our life and also adds to the joy of living.

—REVEREND DALE E. TURNER (1917–2006)

YOU ARE A BLESSING

Even as you walk through these shadows,
you are a blessing to those around you.

—NANCY TUPPER LING

FOR AS LONG AS IT MATTERS

Here's the thing.
In every life crisis, there's that moment
when you must choose whether
to trade down to despair, or up to joy.
I will choose joy.
From now on,
with whatever I've got left,
I'll look for occasions of laughter.
I'll blow soap bubbles
and run barefoot on the beach.
I'll make a list of things to laugh at.
Maybe I'll even dye my hair red.
When I talk, I'll smile.
I'll see that there is always laughter in my voice.
Everyday.
As long as I have.
As long as it matters,
I'll choose joy.

—DOROTHY WILHELM

Author Index

Permissions and Acknowledgments

Grateful acknowledgment is made to the authors and publishers for the use of the following material. Every effort has been made to contact original sources. If notified, the publishers will be pleased to rectify an omission in future editions.

Joan Marie Arbogast for "Steadfast Hope." www.joanmariearbogast.com

Martha K. Baker for "Rx."

Coleman Barks for "The Guest House" by Jalal Al-Din Rumi from *The Essential Rumi*, translated by Coleman Barks, published by Harper-SanFrancisco. Copyright ©1995 by Coleman Barks. Reprinted by kind permission of Coleman Barks. www.colemanbarks.com

Heather Berry for "Tomorrow."

Gwyneth M. Bledsoe for "Lines in the Sand" and "Where There Is…" www.gwynethbledsoe.com

Abigail Brandt for "Renaissance."

Susanne Wiggins Bunch for "For Such a Time as This" and "Tomorrow

Is Not Promised."

Pamela Burke for "I Live in Wonder."

Janine Canan for "Reflect." www.janinecanan.com

Kirsten Casey for "Don't Give Up."

Sally Clark for "The Journey." www.sallyclark.info

SuzAnne C. Cole for "The Gifts of Illness" and "Pain."

Deborah Gordon Cooper for "Prayer in Time of Trouble."

June Cotner for "Perspective." www.junecotner.com

Jim Croegaert for "Like Jacob in the Morning," "Live Quietly," and "Prayer from a Hospital Bed." www.roughstonesmusic.com

Barbara Crooker for "For a Friend Lying in Intensive Care Waiting for Her White Blood Cells to Rejuvenate after a Bone-Marrow Transplant," and "For We Are Here." www.barbaracrooker.com

Phyllis Joy Davison for "A Life Jacket."

Corrine De Winter for "If," "Only Through Surrender," "Small Graces Come to Us," and "Somehow." www.corrinedewinter.com

Barb Dodge for "Angel Promise" by Sara Sanderson.

Annie Dougherty for "Angel Wings."

Virginia Lynn Eathorne for "In the Midst of Pain."

Lori Eberhardy for "Angel Embrace," "The Essence of Touch," "Great Expectations," "A Quiet Comfort," and "Safe Passage."

Charles Ghigna for "The Final Score." www.fathergoose.com

Father John B. Giuliani for "To the Gardener of the World."

Michael S. Glaser for "A Thousand Angels." www.michaelsglaser.com

Ingrid Goff-Maidoff for "God Spoke Today in Flowers," "Grace," "If I Could," and "Now." www.tendingjoy.com

Joanie Guggenmos for "So Very Blessed."

Maryanne Hannan for "A Meditation on Acceptance," "The Way of All Flesh," and "Why Not?" www.mhannan.com

Emily Ruth Hazel for "Life Cannot Be Choreographed" and "Psalm." www.facebook.com/emilyruthhazel

Gary W. Huffman for "Facing the Facts," "Hanging by a Thread," "Restoration Zone," "Sowing, Reaping," "Stubborn Faith," "Take My Hand," and "Testing, Testing..." by Margaret Anne Huffman.

Anita Jepson-Gilbert for "Spring Is My Faith" by Ida Fasel.

Stephanie Kaza for "Letting Go," excerpted from *The Attentive Heart: Conversation with Trees* by Stephanie Kaza. Copyright ©1993 by Stephanie Kaza, published by Ballantine Books. Used by kind permission of Stephanie Kaza.

Susan Koefod for "Patience." www.susankoefod.com

Susan Landon for "Your Monumental Kindness."

"Arlene Gay Levine" for "For a Dear One at a Dark Time," "The Best We Can Do," "This I Know," and "Twilight Cure." www.arlenegaylevine.com

Nancy Tupper Ling for "Blessed," "Breathe Deeply," "Dear Friend," "A New Song," "It Is in the Darkness," "Sweet Child," "This Day," and "You Are a Blessing." www.nancytupperling.com

Joyce Lombard for "Be Curious." www.joycelombard.com

Jill Noblit MacGregor for "From Your Friend."

Peter Markus for "In Sickness."

Sylvia Masi for "3 AM."

Barb Mayer for "Faith Is the Certainty," "Gratitude," "Healing Is Not Only a Question," "Prayer, with a Dose of Hope," and "Take Time."

www.barbmayer.com

Reverend Phyllis Ann Min for "See the Good." www.phylliswithjoy.com

Rosie Molinary for "Breast Cancer Benefit." www.rosiemolinary.com

Jim Moon for "Hope from a Cancer Survivor" by Susan Moon.

Lalita Noronha for "Hope." www.lalitanoronha.com

Susan Rogers Norton for "Grief" and "Sanctuary."

Marian Olson for "Woman to Woman."

Heather Parkins for "Peace Begins Within" and "Rainbows."

Patricia M. Poland for "Still Waters."

Thomas L. Reid for "Hope Will Come Again."

Kate Robinson for "Grace."

Sally Rosloff for "A Good Prognosis."

John Runyard for "To a Dear Friend" by Gwen Tremain Runyard.

Marion Schoeberlein for "Each Day You Call My Heart, O God."

Rabbi Rami M. Shapiro for "For Healing," "Surrender to Wonder,"
    and "Unending Love." www.rabbirami.com

Joan Shroyer-Keno for "Steps."

Molly Srode for "Permanent Gifts."

Cassie Premo Steele for "In the House of the Sun."
    www.cassiepremosteele.com

Paula Timpson for "Get Well," "May You Be Well," and "Stay Well."
    www.paulaspoetryworld.blogspot.com

Dorothy Wilhelm for "For as Long as It Matters."
    www.itsnevertoolate.com

About the Author

June Cotner is the author or editor of thirty books, including the bestselling *Graces, Bedside Prayers,* and *House Blessings.* Her books altogether have sold nearly one million copies and have been featured in many national publications, including *USA Today, Woman's Day,* and *Family Circle.* June has appeared on national television and radio programs.

June's latest love and avocation is giving presentations on "Adopting Prisoner-Trained Shelter Dogs." In 2011, she adopted Indy, a chocolate Lab/Doberman mix (a LabraDobie!), from the Freedom Tails program at Stafford Creek Corrections Center in Aberdeen, Washington. June works with Indy daily to build on the wonderful obedience skills he mastered in the program. She and Indy have appeared on the television shows *AM Northwest* (Portland, OR) and *New Day Northwest* (Seattle).

A graduate of the University of California at Berkeley, June is the mother of two grown children and lives in Poulsbo, Washington, with her husband. Her hobbies include yoga, hiking, paper crafting, and playing with her two grandchildren.

For more information, please visit June's website at www.junecotner.com.

Author photograph by Barb Mayer Photography

Praise for *Get Well Wishes*

"The author of *Graces* and *Bedside Prayers* presents an evocative gift collection...to comfort those who are ill, in the hospital, or recovering from injury or surgery, providing encouragement, inspiration, acceptance, nurturing, and hope to loved ones facing a difficult time in their lives."

—*Forecast Reviews*

"*Get Well Wishes* contains material appropriate for any religion, as well as words appropriate to highlight and brighten an ordinary day...this anthology is one you'll give to friends who may be ill...it is beautifully produced, well-indexed and of a welcoming size to hold easily. Highly recommended."

—Linda Hutton, Hutton Publications

"This anthology of healing thoughts, from a wide range of sources, offers words for those situations when words are hard to find—when someone's in pain or facing serious illness."

—*NAPRA Review*

"These meditations offer rich food for thought on the nature of pain and suffering in the human experience."

—Beliefnet.com

"Meant to be given to an ailing friend, this little book of poetry, prayers, and quotations is packing with words of comfort, faith, courage, and hope…Cotner's selection is wide-ranging enough to include solace from St. Teresa of Avila and advice from Andrew Weil."

—Mike Maza, *The Dallas Morning News*

"A small book filled with poems, prayers, and blessings to buoy the spirits during an illness, *Get Well Wishes* contains offering from Scripture and well-known writers whose short messages, I believe, will some day become classics."

—Bill Duncan, *The News-Review Senior Times*

"A wonderful new book of prayers. The selections are drawn from a variety of spiritual and secular texts. Some contributors will be familiar to you, but many others may be new.

—*Grace Episcopal Church Prayer Network*

TO OUR READERS

Viva Editions publishes books that inform, enlighten, and entertain. We do our best to bring you, the reader, quality books that celebrate life, inspire the mind, revive the spirit, and enhance lives all around. Our authors are practical visionaries: people who offer deep wisdom in a hopeful and helpful manner. Viva was launched with an attitude of growth and we want to spread our joy and offer our support and advice where we can to help you live the Viva way: vivaciously!

We're grateful for all our readers and want to keep bringing you books for inspired living. We invite you to write to us with your comments and suggestions, and what you'd like to see more of. You can also sign up for our online newsletter to learn about new titles, author events, and special offers.

Viva Editions
2246 Sixth St.
Berkeley, CA 94710
www.vivaeditions.com
(800) 780-2279
Follow us on Twitter @vivaeditions
Friend/fan us on Facebook